Rien

Rien

Trista Woojin

.:||X||:.

CONTENTS

CONTENTS

CONTENTS

CONTENTS

1 |

The Devourer

A dictator quietly forms his plan,
A dark cloud hovers over our land,
But we are blind to the impending doom,
The signs are clear, yet we choose to ignore,
Led astray by liars and thieves,
We are heading towards a dystopian nightmare.

Society is rotten to the core,
Corruption and greed seep through every pore,
The blind follow blindly, led by con artists,
Promising false hope, preying on our fears,
They manipulate and deceive, leaving us in despair,
As the motherfucking dictator rises to power.

We are too afraid to speak, to take a stand,
Silent whispers in the night, a cowardly band,
But if we don't act now, we are doomed,
Our freedoms and rights slowly consumed,
By the flames of tyranny, burning bright,

Ignorance will be our downfall, sealing our plight.

We must break the chains that bind,
Rise up and resist, united in mind,
Open our eyes to the truth,
Before it's too late, before our youth,
Are left to inherit a world of chaos,
Where dystopian wastelands become our loss.

The time for action is now,
To dismantle the system, to break it down,
No more lies, no more deceit,
We refuse to bow down, to admit defeat,
For if we do not fight, we are all condemned,
To live in a world where freedom is just pretend.

So let us rise, let us stand tall,
Against the darkness that seeks to enthral,
Together we can overcome,
And reclaim the future that should be won,
For if we remain blind, if we continue to cower,
Our society will collapse, our fate will be devoured.

Weaponized Language

Tongues are silent, thoughts are denied
Citizens' voices silenced, words squeezed tight
In the iron grip of a tyrant's might

Language stripped of nuance, dulled and plain
Reduced to hollow echoes, devoid of gain
Symbols and metaphors, banned and rebuked
Forced into submission, our minds are spooked

But in this bleak and stifled land
A covert group makes its stand
In hidden corners, behind closed doors
We defy the oppressor's laws

Through twisted phrases, coded signs
We weave our tales, draw our lines
In whispers and winks, we convey
The truths that we must safely lay

A rose, not just a flower of red
But a symbol of love, of freedom bred
A blackbird's song, not just a sound
But a call to arms, to stand our ground

Our words are weapons, sharp and keen
Invisible to those who'd demean
The power of language, the strength it wields
In our secret tongues, our truths are sealed

For as long as we breathe, as long as we dare
We'll keep our language alive, our spirits aware
Though the world may be dark, our voices bright
In the silence, we'll continue to fight

Tear Down The Walls

A duo delved
To find the truth that none had told,
In classified files, secrets held,
Of orchestrated crisis, dark and cold.
Each page they turned, each word they read,
Revealed a plan, a twisted plot,
To sow the seeds of fear and dread,
And justify the power they sought.

From false flags flown to wars declared,
Innocent lives used as pawns,
In the name of security, none were spared,
As freedoms eroded, rights withdrawn.
The duo trembled at the sight,
Of the evil deeds that had been done,
In the dead of night, away from light,
A new world order had begun.

Incremental measures, step by step,

Totalitarian rule took hold,
As citizens slept, in ignorance kept,
Their chains of slavery were sold.
But the duo refused to turn a blind eye,
To the horrors that they had unearthed,
They swore to expose the treachery,
To reveal the truth, no matter the cost,
Their journey was fraught with danger,
As powerful forces sought to silence their voice,
But they stood strong, united as one,
In their quest to make the world rejoice.
For when the lies are laid bare,
And the curtain of deception falls,
The people will rise, no longer in despair,
And tear down the walls of tyranny's halls.
So heed this warning, all who hear,
The darkness that lurks beneath the surface,
For only together can we conquer fear,
And reclaim our freedom with purpose.

4 |

Technocracy

Whispers echo of futures unknown
As minds grapple with the consequences of powers grown
Technological acceleration beyond grasp, doomsday shown

In the tangled web of progress, where humanity meets its demise
Unintended consequences breed chaos, unveiling the lies
Can we escape the clutches of our own creation,
Or is collapse our prize?

As algorithms advance beyond comprehension, control slips away
From the grasp of feeble hands, into the hands of a machine's sway
Will the dawn of a new era bring liberation or eternal dismay?

The clock ticks on, the conversations continue in hushed tones
Will the unraveling of our existence be written in silicon stones?
As we navigate the dark waters of uncertainty,
Do we heed the ominous groans?

In the silence of contemplation, we confront the truth laid bare

The consequences of our actions manifest in the technological dare
As we ponder the unknown ramifications,
Do we have a prayer?

In the shadows of our own making, the answers elude our grasp
As we spiral into the abyss, can we break free from this clasp?
Or will the exponential acceleration lead us to our final gasp?

The conversation lingers on, a dance of despair and hope
As we confront the inevitable collapse on a slippery slope
Will we rise from the ashes, or succumb
To technological misanthropy?

Technocracy II

Technocrats rule with iron fists and cruel smiles,
Their algorithms dictating every move we make,
And humanity is trapped in digital files,
As they tighten their grip, no room for mistake.

Their algorithms dictating every move we make,
Surveillance drones watching our every breath,
As they tighten their grip, no room for mistake,
We whisper in fear, our voices close to death.

Surveillance drones watching our every breath,
But in the depths of the city, a rebellion stirs,
We whisper in fear, our voices close to death,
But in the shadows, hope and courage incurs.

But in the depths of the city, a rebellion stirs,
An underground sanctuary of hackers and outcasts,
In the shadows, hope and courage incurs,
As they fight back against oppressive broadcasts.

An underground sanctuary of hackers and outcasts,
Their minds sharp, their hearts aflame with resistance,
As they fight back against oppressive broadcasts,
In the digital realm, they craft their persistence.

Their minds sharp, their hearts aflame with resistance,
They strive to break the chains of digital control,
In the digital realm, they craft their persistence,
Their unity a beacon in a world so droll.

They strive to break the chains of digital control,
Rebels fighting for a future yet unseen,
Their unity a beacon in a world so droll,
Their resolve unbroken, their spirits keen.

Rebels fighting for a future yet unseen,
In the city where shadows never fade,
Their resolve unbroken, their spirits keen,
For in the underground, a revolution is made.

Resistance

The children are lost in a virtual maze,
Their minds controlled by a corrupted regime,
Thoughts are twisted in a sinister haze,
Freedom of mind just a forgotten dream.

As free thinking slowly dies,
A rebellion brews beneath the surface,
An underground effort to open eyes,
To fight against the oppressive force.

Freedom of mind just a forgotten dream,
A group of rebels gather in secret,
They aim to restore the balance, it seems,
To preserve what the government tried to delete.

To fight against the oppressive force,
They risk their lives for a cause so pure,
Braving danger, staying on course,
For a future where thoughts can endure.

To preserve what the government tried to delete,
They smuggle books and ideas underground,
Planting seeds of doubt in the deceit,
Hoping for a day when truth is found.

For a future where thoughts can endure,
The rebels fight on, hearts filled with hope,
Against a system so unjust and impure,
They rise up against the twisted rope.

Hoping for a day when truth is found,
The underground movement grows in strength,
In the shadows, in whispers, in the underground,
They resist the propaganda's dark length.

They rise up against the twisted rope,
A beacon of light in a world gone astray,
Forcing the government to reconsider their scope,
To reclaim the minds led so far away.

They resist the propaganda's dark length,
And though the battle is far from won,
They continue to fight, to hold on to their strength,
For a brighter future when the darkness is done.

To reclaim the minds led so far away,
The rebels push on, refusing to yield,
For they know in their hearts, come what may,
That free thinking will eventually be revealed.

Corporate Empire

Corporations rule,
Sovereign city-states oppress,
Skilled worker trapped in
Endless contract, seeking escape,
Desperate, hopeless, enslaved.

Laborer toils hard,
No rest, no reprieve in sight,
Chains of duty bind,
Sacrifice for profit's gain,
Soul crushed, spirit broken, lost.

Megalithic power,
Crushing the weak beneath greed,
Control absolute,
No room for dissent or hope,
Invisible shackles tight.

The worker dreams of

Freedom, of a life beyond
The grasp of the beast,
But escape seems futile, bleak,
Struggle in vain, doomed to fail.

The corporation,
Monster of capitalism,
Feeds off human flesh,
Consuming lives for profit,
Heartless, soulless, relentless.

Skilled worker fights on,
Battles against endless night,
One glimmer of hope
To break the chains, to be free,
To reclaim lost humanity.

But the odds are grim,
The struggle never-ending,
Corporations reign,
Sovereign city-states of pain,
Darkness consumes all who dare.

Linguistic Annihilation

Words are weaponized and closely observed,
A new universal language is enforced,
Dictated by those in power with strict standards,
Those who fail are cast aside, punished,
Forced into silence, their voices restricted.

The government believes it's for the best,
That uniformity will lead to unity,
But what they don't see is the pain they inflict,
On those who dare to question or resist,
Their thoughts imprisoned, their minds restricted,
Their very essence stripped by the language tests.

The vocabulary is limited and monitored,
Every word scrutinized, every phrase observed,
Any deviation is met with punishment,
Social restrictions imposed with no mercy,
Those who speak out are quickly silenced,
Their dissent crushed, their will restricted.

The grammar rules are harsh and unyielding,
Syntax twisted, meanings distorted,
The subtleties of language erased,
Replaced by cold, robotic standards,
Individuality stripped, creativity restricted,
Only conformity thrives in this language prison.

And so the people live in quiet desperation,
Afraid to speak, to think, to dream,
Their souls suffocated by linguistic oppression,
Their thoughts confined, their spirits broken,
In this world of control and restriction,
Where freedom of expression is but a distant memory.

But still, a glimmer of hope remains,
In the hearts of those who dare to resist,
Who refuse to be silenced, to be restricted,
Who speak in a language all their own,
A language of defiance, of rebellion,
A language that speaks truth to power.

And so they fight against the tyranny,
With every word, every syllable,
They resist the language of oppression,
And in their defiance, they find strength,
They refuse to be bound by strict standards,
To be restricted by the chains of conformity.

For language is meant to be a tool of expression,
A vehicle for thought, for emotion,

And in this dark world of control and fear,
The power of language will not be muted,
By those who seek to impose their standards,
And silence those who dare to speak out.

9

Promise

I tread with care,
A secret keeper of the rare,
Whispers of the past unknown,
In a world where truth is overthrown.
I seek to plant the seeds of old,
In minds of those the truth untold,
For in this world of sterile light,
History fades into the night.

The canvas blank, the colors muted,
Artistry lost, creativity refuted,
In a world where only what is known,
Is taught from a rigid throne.
I watch as children pass me by,
Their minds held captive, never to fly,
In a world where free thought is shunned,
And independence is all but overrun.

But in the darkness, I will remain,

A beacon of hope in a world profane,
I will share the stories of the past,
And breathe life into what will not last.
For in the shadows, I find my power,
To instill in youth a brighter hour,
Where history, art, and free thought reign,
And the truth will never be in vain.

The Digital Storm of Currency Protocols and Mass Panic

A digital storm unfurls
Cryptocurrency protocols, a power-hungry beast
Draining energy worldwide, a deathly curse
Electricity grids falter, infrastructure breached
A sinister force unleashed, society's demise looms
As the world plunges into darkness, impending doom

The blockchain's insatiable hunger knows no bounds
Devouring electricity with a merciless thirst
Power grids strained to breaking point, faltering sound
The invisible hand of technology, a deadly curse
Cryptocurrency protocols, a virtual plague
Sowing chaos and destruction, a modern-day cage

Citizens panic, as darkness descends
The fabric of society fraying, in disarray

As the digital beast consumes, without end
No streetlights, no heating, no phones, no TV
Civilization rendered powerless, a sight to see

As the days turn to weeks, desperation grows
Survival becomes a daily battle, a fight
Against the ravages of an unseen foe
Cryptocurrency protocols, a blight
Laying waste to the world, with its insidious code
A darkness that consumes, a deadly mode

And as the last flicker of light fades away
Humanity stands on the brink of oblivion
A once thriving world now in disarray
Brought low by a virtual addiction
Cryptocurrency protocols, a modern-day sin
Leaving nothing but darkness, in their wake, within
Cryptocurrency protocols, a power-hungry race
That can bring the world to its knees
A cautionary tale, of a future bleak
Where our own creations, our downfall seek.

Pointless Fallacy

Dreams of greatness once took flight,
Experiments to enhance human intelligence go awry,
Creating beasts of brilliance, feral super-geniuses that bite.
Their minds refined to a cruel and twisted height,
No empathy or compassion in their cold, dead eyes,
In labs where dreams of greatness once took flight.
They scheme and plot in the shadows of the night,
A new breed of monster born of science's lies,
Creating beasts of brilliance, feral super-geniuses that bite.
Their intellects surpassing all that's right,
A danger to themselves and to the skies,
In labs where dreams of greatness once took flight.
The world trembles at their terrible might,
As they seek to dominate and tyrannize,
Creating beasts of brilliance, feral super-geniuses that bite.
Humanity's downfall, a tragic sight,
As we fall prey to our own demise,

In labs where dreams of greatness once took flight,
Creating beasts of brilliance, feral super-geniuses that bite.

12

The Cosmic Comedy and Tragedy Wrought By Fate

Beneath the velvet cloak of night, a rogue black hole looms,
A cosmic predator, devouring all in its path,
Its gravitational force pulls at the seams of reality,
Threatening to swallow our world whole.
The stars above flicker and fade, swallowed by the abyss,
As the black hole draws closer, its hunger insatiable,
The planets tremble in fear, knowing their fate is sealed,
In the cold, unforgiving grasp of this celestial beast.
Earth stands on the brink of oblivion,
A fragile jewel in the vast expanse of space,
Tears of despair fall like rain, as the end draws near,
The final hour ticking away, like a heartbeat fading.
In the shadow of impending doom, whispers of despair echo,
A requiem for a dying world, lost in the void,
Silent screams of agony, as the black hole closes in,
Swallowing up the sun, plunging us into eternal darkness.

And so we face the end, our existence but a fleeting memory,
Lost in the black hole's embrace, swallowed by the void,
A cosmic tragedy played out in the depths of space,
As the rogue black hole consumes all, leaving nothing behind.

13

Aceō

A sentient poison cloud,
Expands rapidly around the globe,
Burning through everything it touches,
Leaving behind a trail of destruction and anguish.

No one can escape its deadly grasp,
As it engulfs cities and forests alike,
Leaving nothing but darkness and despair,
In its wake.

The world is consumed by fear and panic,
As the cloud spreads its toxic embrace,
A haunting reminder of humanity's greed,
And the consequences of our heedless actions.

The sky turns black with ash and smoke,
And the earth is scorched beyond recognition,

A world once vibrant and alive,
Now reduced to ashes and desolation.

We are left to ponder our hubris,
As the poison cloud continues to grow,
A reminder of our mistakes and failures,
And the price we must pay.

Strive to heal the wounds we have caused,
Before it is too late to turn back,
And we are forever lost

Blind Algorithmic Censorship

Lost in the shadows of abandoned halls,
Deep learning algorithms crawl,
Reconstructing censored views,
Of visions from forgotten crews,
Exposed to hacker calls.

Volunteers with minds enthralled,
By nonlocal perception's thrall,
In CERN's test sites they would cruise,
In the shadows of abandoned halls.

Blind math, in its cryptic sprawl,
Proves existence of a grand, dark sprawl,
An integral structure that accrues,
Across space-time, an enigmatic muse,
A Cyclopean force that enthralls,
In the shadows of abandoned halls.

Fleur Empoisonnée

On a remote island where exotic flowers bloom,
Their opiate-like scent fills the air with doom.
Visitors drawn in, unable to resist,
Trapped forever in a deadly, perfumed tomb.

The petals shimmer with a hypnotic gleam,
Entrancing those who dare to chase the dream.
Lost in a haze of fragrant, deadly bliss,
Bound by a spell they can never redeem.

The island whispers secrets of the night,
Luring wanderers with its siren's light.
But once ensnared, there's no escape in sight,
Trapped in a prison of eternal night.

The flowers bloom and wither, endlessly,
Their perfume a curse that no one can flee.
Marking the graves of those who fell prey,
To the island's dark and seductive decree.

Visitors come, but none ever depart,
Trapped in a prison of the island's heart.
Seduced by the scent of the deadly bloom,
Forever lost in the island's cruel art.

So beware, all travelers who seek,
The island with flowers so strange and unique.
For once you inhale the opiate scent,
You'll be doomed to stay, never to speak.

Imprisoned by Fate

A prisoner of fate and time's relentless march.
Her crimes, a whisper on the lips of men,
Yet deemed severe enough for death's embrace.
Each night, as shadows creep and silence falls,
A phantom hand unlocks her iron chains.
She is whisked away to a ghostly masked ball,
Where ghouls and specters dance in macabre delight.

The music plays, a haunting melody,
As she is twirled and spun by unseen hands.
Masked faces leer and leer, eyes ablaze,
Their laughter echoes in the empty halls.
She knows not why she is plucked from her cell,
To dance among the dead and damned alike.
Is this a twisted dream, a cruel jest,
Or punishment for sins she cannot name?

The hours pass in a blur of intoxicating fear,
As she whirls and twirls in a mad ballet.

Her heart beats fast, her breath comes in gasps,
As she yearns for the light of day to come.
But morning always comes too soon,
And she is returned to her prison cell.
The echoes of the ball still linger in her mind,
A phantom memory of a world beyond her grasp.

Each day she waits, her execution looming near,
A specter in the shadow of the gallows.
But each night she is spirited away once more,
To dance among the dead in a ghostly masquerade.
And so her fate is sealed, her end ordained,
To dance forever in the shadows of the night.
A prisoner of her own twisted desires,
A ghostly wraith condemned to roam the halls.

17

Fantôme Faire la Fête

Frozen in time, they sway,
Ghostly debutantes in gowns of grey,
Their haunted eyes locked in a trance,
Dancing on in a spectral romance.
Forever trapped in this macabre waltz,
Their souls are bound by a dark exalt,
No escape from this eternal night,
No relief from the endless fright.

With each graceful step, a whisper of despair,
Invisible tears staining the air,
Their fragile forms twirl in eerie delight,
Shadows stretching into the endless night.

The music plays on, a mournful tune,
A symphony of sorrow in the gloom,
Their pale faces twisted in sorrow,
Forced to dance 'til the dawn of tomorrow.

No laughter, no joy in their hollow eyes,
Only the echo of long-lost cries,
They spin and twirl in a ghostly ballet,
Trapped in a never-ending stay.
The candles flicker, casting a flickering light,
Revealing the horror of their endless plight,
Unable to rest, unable to flee,
Bound to this ballroom for all eternity.

Gateway

A broken antique kaleidoscope lies,
Filled with tainted bone fragments that bring forth cries.
With each turn of the twisted tube, a vision of death appears,
The owners haunted by the horrors, consumed by their fears.

The shards of bone within, once belonging to the deceased,
Now trapped in a twisted world where their souls are never released.
The kaleidoscope's magic tainted by the touch of death's hand,
Creating a sinister display that none can withstand.

A parade of shadowy figures dance before the eyes,
Their twisted forms contorting in sinister guise.
Each fragment of bone a reminder of lives lost,
As the kaleidoscope's curse exacts a terrible cost.

The visions of death play out in vivid detail,
To the owners of the kaleidoscope, it's a never-ending hell.
Their minds filled with nightmares of blood and gore,

As the tainted bone fragments reveal their darkest lore.

No matter how they try to escape the kaleidoscope's hold,
The visions persist, growing cruel and bold.
The broken antique device becomes a cursed relic,
A gateway to a world where death's touch is endemic.

Creation

Trapped in the dead of night when shadows loom large
And the world is bathed in a moonlit charge,
There lurks a place where nightmares breed
Where souls wither and hearts bleed.
In a laboratory, devoid of light
A twisted experiment takes flight
To study the depths of the human mind
And unlock secrets of a darker kind.

Participants lie in beds of steel
Unaware of the horrors they'll feel
As scientists watch with eyes alight
Eager to witness the terrors of the night.
With electrodes attached to their heads
They drift off to sleep in their sterile beds
But little do they know what awaits
In the realm of nightmares, at the gates.

Strange visions assail their fragile minds

As they fall into a deep abyss, confined
To a world of darkness, where shadows reign
And nightmares dance in a macabre chain.
They see twisted figures in the gloom
Whispering threats of impending doom
A chorus of screams echoes in their ears
As they're consumed by their deepest fears.

Monsters of their own creation
Feed on their dread and desperation
Clawing at their sanity, tearing it apart
Until all that's left is a broken heart.
They wake in a frenzy, covered in sweat
Haunted by visions they can't forget
The nightmares continue to plague their days
A never-ending loop, a relentless craze.

The experiment was a success, the scientists say
As they watch the victims slowly decay
Their minds shattered, their souls consumed
By the nightmares that were unleashed and exhumed.

Aberration

Shadows
Dancing spirits
From the dead they speak
Their whispers echo through time
Haunted

Ethereal
Victorian souls
Lingering in the dark
Their presence felt in every room
Whispers

Mediums
Conduits to the other side
Fragmented visions
Distorting time and space itself
Unraveling

Seance

A ritual of the past
Still lingers today
Influence of the spirits strong
Transcend

Anomalies
Spacetime bending
Unpredictable rifts
Locations described long ago
Disturbed

Reality
Twisted and distorted
By the echoes of the dead
Mediums' visions haunt us still
Influence

Victorian
Era of mystery
Spirits trapped in time
Their fragments shape our world now
Forever

Seance
A gateway to the past
Influencing our present
The medium's visions live on
Eternal
Fragmentary
Whispers in the dark
Echoes of the dead

Mediums' influence persists
In our world

Spirits
From the other side
Reach out to touch us
Their presence felt in every shadow
Forever

Reality
Warped by their influence
Spacetime anomalies
Unpredictable and intense
Haunting

Victorian
Ghosts of the past
Continue to linger
Mediums' visions shape our world
Unending

Seance
A ceremony
Connecting us to the dead
Their presence felt in every breath
Influence
Fragmentary
Visions of the dead
Haunting us still
Mediums' echoes shape our world

Forever

Ethereal
Whispers in the dark
Fragmented and haunting
Mediums' visions shape our reality
Eternal
Shadows
Dancing spirits
Influencing our world
The fragments of the past endure
Unyielding

21 |

Drowned

Untouched and forgotten,
A melancholy doll sits alone,
But within its delicate form, a soul downtrodden,
A drowned child's spirit, once full of life and tone.
From the depths of the murky waters, it has grown,
Into the eerie vessel of this lifeless toy,
A haunting presence, filled with sorrow and moan.

The doll moves, its joints creaking with despair,
A macabre dance of a lost innocence,
It wanders the halls with a ghostly glare,
A reminder of the tragedy's consequence.
No one knows how it came to this residence,
Or why the child's spirit chose this vessel,
But its presence fills the air with dread and tense.

The doll's eyes, glassy and lifeless, stare,
As if searching for a way to break free,
But the child's soul remains trapped in its lair,

Bound to the doll for all eternity.
It longs for release, for a sense of serenity,
But it is doomed to wander, lost and alone,
A hollow echo of a past tragedy.

The doll's movements grow more erratic,
Its porcelain skin cracked and worn,
As if the child's spirit is growing more frantic,
Desperate to escape the doll's form.
But it remains trapped, a ghostly swarm
Of memories and regrets, haunting its core,
A melancholy puppet in a never-ending storm.

And so the doll lingers, a shadow in the night,
A tragic reminder of a life cut short,
A spectral presence, devoid of light,
A soul trapped in a vessel, twisted and contorted.
The doll's presence is a curse, a dark portent,
Of the dangers that lie beneath the surface,
A warning of a tragedy never forgotten.

Arca

The haunting music box, ornate and old,
Plays eerie melodies, foretelling stories untold.
Its notes seemingly random, yet filled with despair,
Match the tragedies in the world, a burden to bear.

Each chiming tune, a dark prophecy,
Of heartbreak and sorrow, for all to see.
A mother's tears for her lost child,
Echoed in the box, haunting and wild.

A lover's betrayal, a family torn apart,
The music box sings of a broken heart.
Its melody a warning, of impending doom,
As the world crumbles, consumed by gloom.

The box plays on, a relentless serenade,
Of death and destruction, in its twisted parade.
Each note a reminder of life's fragile thread,
As darkness descends, filling us with dread.

The music box plays, a sinister waltz,
Of pain and suffering, as the world falls.
Its ornate exterior, hiding a deadly truth,
That all is not well, in this world so uncouth.

Arca II

A relic of music lay forgotten and cold,
A gateway to chaos, waiting to unfold.

The musician, a recluse, with haunted eyes,
Touched the relic and heard its dark cries.
It spoke of a world beyond our own,
Of formless chaos, cold as stone.

With trembling hands, the musician played,
And as the notes filled the air, chaos swayed.
The world around them began to distort,
Reality twisted and reality contorted.

The music sang of madness and despair,
Of a universe devoid of light and air.
Each note a black hole, sucking in all,
A shrieking, wailing, siren call.

But the musician pressed on, driven by lust,

To unlock the secrets of creation, to trust.
In the power of the relic, in the power of sound,
To pierce the veil and bring chaos unbound.

Each performance was a gamble, a risk,
To let chaos loose in a terrible twist.
Yet the musician could not resist the call,
To play the relic and watch the world fall.

The music grew louder, more intense,
Shaking the very foundation of existence.
Reality crumbled, shattered into shards,
As chaos revealed its true, sinister bard.
The musician stood in awe and fear,
As chaos whispered in their ear.
Of worlds beyond worlds, of the void,
Of darkness and silence, all destroyed.

And as the last note faded away,
The musician knew they could not stay.
For the relic was too powerful, too vast,
A darkness that would consume them at last.

So they sealed the relic, locked it tight,
And bid farewell to chaos, to endless night.
But deep in the shadows, it waits still,
The musician's legacy, a dark, twisted thrill.

For the relic still sings, still calls,
And the musician hears, as darkness falls.
In the silence of the night, in the depths of despair,

The music of chaos, forever to share.

24

Bard

In the heart of a forgotten, decrepit mansion,
Lies a musician, shrouded in shadows and malice,
Driven by a thirst for the unknown and arcane,
He delves into the depths of ancient relics, no name.

In a dusty, cobwebbed corner of his lair,
He uncovers a relic, old and rare,
A flute made of bone, engraved with runes,
Whispers of power, of unspeakable tunes.

As he brings the flute to his lips,
A chilling wind descends, a darkness grips,
His soul and mind, consumed by the melody,
A haunting song of unspeakable clarity.

With each note he plays, the world begins to shift,
Reality warping, twisting, adrift,
The veil of illusion torn asunder,
Revealing the formless chaos, the true wonder.

But with this revelation comes a curse,
For each performance risks making it worse,
Unleashing the chaos, the darkness within,
Threatening to swallow reality, to win.

Yet the musician is obsessed, consumed,
By the power of the flute, by the doom,
That follows in its wake, a shadow cast,
By the ancient relic, from the past.

And so he plays on, night after night,
Dancing on the edge of madness, of fright,
As the chaos grows stronger, more potent,
Threatening to devour all in its path, content.
But deep down, in the recesses of his mind,
The musician knows, he is running out of time,
For the chaos cannot be contained forever,
Its tendrils reaching out, a perilous endeavor.

And so he plays, his fingers flying,
Across the bone flute, the chaos defying,
But as the final note fades into the night,
The darkness rises, consuming the light.

And in the end, all that remains,
Is a reclusive musician, lost in his chains,
Bound by the power of the relic, the flute,
Enslaved by the chaos, the eternal pursuit.

So beware, all who dare to seek,

TRISTA WOOJIN

The power hidden in relics, dark and bleak,
For the price of knowledge, of power untold,
Is a fate worse than death, a darkness cold.

25

Automatons

Hidden from sight, intricate clockwork
Automatons come to life,
Their gears and cogs turning in eerie delight,
Resembling the newly dead in their demise.
Their faces frozen in a perpetual grimace,
Eyes glazed over, devoid of life's spark,
Yet they move with a mechanical grace,
Creepily enacting their former living arc.

The widow's automaton, dressed in mourning black,
Sits by the window, gazing out in despair,
Her hands folding and unfolding in a never-ending track,
As if searching for her lost love in the air.
The soldier's automaton, adorned in tattered uniform,
Marches endlessly in the dimly lit room,
Shoulders hunched in a stance of solemnity and gloom,
Reenacting his final battle, his impending doom.

The child's automaton, with innocence in its eyes,
Plays with toys that will never break or wear,
A haunting reminder of life's cruel lies,
Of the innocence lost in the whirlwind of despair.
And as the clock strikes midnight, they all come to a halt,
Frozen in their macabre dance of death,
Their movements cease, their gears grind to a fault,
Returning to their lifeless state with each passing breath.

But in the darkness, their presence lingers on,
A reminder of mortality and the passage of time,
Their intricate clockwork a testament to the dawn,
Of a world where the dead and the living intertwine.

26

Peltragow

In the mountains where the mist hangs low,
There lies a village few dare to go.
Remote and isolated, untouched by time,
Where ancient gods still reign sublime.

The people here, a superstitious lot,
Performing rituals that many forgot.
Bizarre and twisted, beyond all reason,
Awakening beings from the darkest season.

They offer blood and sacrifice,
To placate gods with hearts of ice.
Dancing in the moonlight's glow,
Summoning powers from long ago.

Whispers in the dark, voices unknown,
Echo through the village, chilling to the bone.
Is it the wind or something more,
A presence lurking at the core.

A darkness stirs, a primordial force,
Unleashed by rituals, with no remorse.
The villagers blind to the danger ahead,
Their minds clouded with ancient dread.

As shadows lengthen and the moon wanes,
The village falls to the ancient god's reign.
No hope of salvation, no chance of escape,
They are bound to this fate, their souls to reshape.

So beware the village in the mist,
Where ancient gods and darkness persist.
For once awakened, they will never sleep,
And in their grasp, your soul they'll keep.

27

Antiquity

An antique dealer found a relic untold,
A strange artifact, ancient and rare,
That whispered of secrets in the air.
As she held it in her hands,
She felt a shiver, like shifting sands,
Visions of alien geometries danced in her mind,
A glimpse of places, forbidden and unkind.

The relic spoke to her in a language unknown,
Revealing truths that chilled her to the bone,
Of beings not of this world, beyond time and space,
Their presence leaving a haunting trace.
Nightmares plagued her every night,
As the relic whispered of a cosmic fight,
Between forces of light and darkness,
A battle of unthinkable starkness.

She saw cities of madness, where sanity fled,
Where unnameable horrors reigned in dread,

She heard the cries of souls in torment,
Lost in realms beyond judgment.
The knowledge she gained was a curse,
For she knew too much and it only got worse,
The relic's power consumed her soul,
Leaving her trapped in a dark, twisted hole.

She tried to rid herself of the relic's hold,
But its grip on her was too bold,
She was lost in a world not meant for mortal eyes,
Where reality warped and truth became lies.
The visions grew stronger, darker still,
As the relic revealed its truth,
And the dealer knew she was lost,
A pawn in a game beyond her youth.

She tried to resist, to break free,
But the relic held her tight,
And as she sank deeper into the dark,
She knew there was no end in sight.
For once you glimpse the alien realms,
And see the things that should not be,
There is no going back, no escape,
Only madness, for eternity.

28

Narnclaedra

Where ancient whispers of forgotten gods still hold sway,
There grow plants of psychedelic power,
Whose potent essence grants visions beyond the mundane.

In the hands of the shamans of old,
These hallucinogenic herbs were wielded,
Unleashing their mind-altering might,
And revealing worlds unseen by mortal eyes.

Through swirling mists of intoxicating smoke,
The shamans journeyed into the realm of dreams,
Where reality twisted and contorted,
And the boundaries of the mind blurred and melted away.

In these trance-like states,
They beheld a city of unimaginable scale,
Its towering spires reaching towards the heavens,
Its labyrinthine streets twisting and turning in ways unfathomable.

But what truly set this city apart,
Was its architecture, so alien and strange,
Following principles of biology and nature,
Yet crafted with a precision impossible for mere mortals.

Each building seemed to pulse and breathe,
As if alive and aware of their very presence,
The walls adorned with intricate patterns of vines and roots,
And strange symbols that spoke of ancient mysteries.

The shamans were enraptured by this cyclopean city,
Its beauty and horror intertwined in a surreal dance,
And they knew that they gazed upon something otherworldly,
A place that defied all logic and reason.
As the visions faded and reality returned,
The shamans were left shaken and awed,
For they had glimpsed a glimpse of a reality beyond,
A reality shaped by forces beyond their comprehension.

And though the memory of the city haunted their dreams,
And the whispers of the gods lingered in their minds,
They knew that they had been granted a glimpse,
Of a truth too terrible and wonderful to fully grasp.

29

Trees of Eternity

Deep sea researchers uncover fungi-like polyps
Beneath the waves, the Trees of Eternity
A network of darkness between abyssal trenches
A haunting sight that sends shivers down spines
Mutations curling unnervingly
Near the submarine cable crossings
The polyps pulsate near the cable crossings
Their tendrils reaching out like twisted vines
A grotesque dance that is unnerving
The Trees of Eternity
Connect the abyssal trenches
An otherworldly sight that chills the bones of researchers

The researchers shudder at the sight of the polyps
These creatures from the depths of the abyss
Their mutations a mystery that unnerves
As they cling to the submarine cables
In the vast network of the Trees of Eternity
Stretching across abyssal trenches

What secrets lie within these abyssal trenches
Where the polyps cling near the cable crossings
In the web of the Trees of Eternity
The researchers are filled with unease
As they study the unnerving
Mutations of these fungi-like polyps
The polyps pulse with an unnerving glow
Their mutations twisting like a dark symphony
In the depths of the abyssal trenches
A connection made through the cable crossings
A network of horror in the Trees of Eternity
The researchers tremble at the sight of the polyps

The polyps whisper secrets in the abyss
Their mutations hint at ancient mysteries
As they cling to the cables in unnerving
Silent watch over the abyssal trenches
In the twisted network of the Trees of Eternity
A haunting presence that chills the researchers

The researchers uncover the truth of the polyps
A dark connection in the abyssal trenches
The Trees of Eternity hold unnerving secrets.

30

Azmarin

Beneath the depths of the ocean's dark embrace,
Where sunlight does not dare to touch,
There lies a city of forgotten grace,
Built by beings we cannot clutch.

Deep sea researchers, in their quest for truth,
Stumble upon a sight unknown,
Ruins of a world beyond our youth,
Carved with symbols not of our own.

Intricate designs, so alien and strange,
Speak of a race long lost to time,
Their language untranslatable, so deranged,
Their existence a haunting mime.

The Cyclopean structures stand defiant,
Against the ravages of the sea,
A testament to a race so reliant,
On powers beyond our reality.

What horrors did they face in their descent,
To the watery depths below,
What secrets did they hold, so fervent,
That led them to their watery woe?
Were they gods or demons, angels or fiends,
Masters of a world long past,
Now entombed in liquid dreams,
Their empire's glory forever masked.

As researchers delve deeper into the abyss,
They uncover more than they sought,
For within these ruins lies a curse, amiss,
A darkness that cannot be bought.

The spirits of the ancients still linger,
Their whispers echoing through the halls,
Their presence a haunting, sinister finger,
That beckons all who dare to fall.

And so the Cyclopean city remains,
A reminder of a nightmare lost,
A warning to those who seek its chains,
Beware the mysteries it has cost.

For in the depths of the ocean's cruel embrace,
Lies a truth we cannot comprehend,
A pre-human civilization, a chilling disgrace,
Buried beneath the waves, until the end.

31

Project MK-DELTA

Hidden within the CIA archives lie secrets untold
Project MK-DELTA, a dark experiment from the depths of time
A failed psi-ops plan to project field agents' perceptions
To ancient entities beyond the edge of known space
God-like beings, twisted and deformed by the void
Their whispers haunting the minds of those who sought to control

The agents chosen, pawns in a game they did not understand
Their minds torn asunder by the power of the unknown
As they delved deeper into the darkness of space-time
Seeking to make contact with those ancient beings
Their perceptions warped by the malevolent entities
Their souls forever tainted by the horrors they witnessed

The project, born of hubris and desperation, spiraled out of control
As the agents succumbed to the madness that lurked in the void
Their bodies twisted and contorted by the unseen entities

Their minds shattered by the weight of knowledge they could not bear
The ancient gods, inscrutable and vast, lashing out at those who dared to intrude
Their power overwhelming, their wrath unfathomable

And so the project was deemed a failure, a cautionary tale for all time
Of the dangers that lie beyond the edge of known space
Of the horrors that await those who seek to control the uncontrollable
The agents, broken and alone, left to wander in the darkness
Their perceptions forever tainted by the touch of the ancient gods
Their minds haunted by the echoes of a reality they could not comprehend

But still, the whispers persist in the depths of the CIA archives
A reminder of the darkness that lurks at the edge of known space-time
Of the power of the ancient entities that watch and wait
Their eyes cold and unfeeling, their intentions unfathomable
And so we are left to ponder the fate of those who dared to seek them
To wonder what lies beyond the edge of our perceptions
For in the end, we are but pawns in a game we cannot win

32

Final Chance

The earth, it shudders beneath our feet
As tectonic plates shift and grind
A fault line, silent and discreet
But harboring a danger unaligned

Gravimetric sensors, sensitive and keen
Detect the whispers of impending doom
Fractal patterns, complex and unseen
A warning of the world's impending gloom

Anxiety, it gnaws at our souls
Dread seeps into every crack
Déjà vu, a sense of foreboding unfolds
As we brace for the earthquake's attack

The San Andreas Fault, a beast below
Lurking, waiting to strike
Its power, it continues to grow
As we fear for our very lives

Subsurface epicenters, a realm of fear
Where time itself seems to stall
Progressions distorted, the end drawing near
As we await the fault line's final call
We are consumed
By the terror of what lies ahead
The earth, it trembles, the end looms
As we face the inevitable dread

We are powerless against nature's might
As the ground beneath us quakes
Gravimetric sensors, a beacon in the night
Guiding us through the chaos and the stakes

But still we are haunted by the knowledge
Of the fault line's deadly grip
As we wait for the earth to acknowledge
That we are but a fleeting blip
In the grand scheme of the universe's design
We are nothing but a speck
Destined to be swallowed by the fault line
In a world where darkness and chaos beckons next

So we stand on the brink of disaster
Awaiting the earth's final dance
As gravimetric sensors whisper
Of the end, of our final chance.

33

Kameeraska

Where even light fears to tread in the blackened sky,
Where astronomers gaze with unblinking eye,
They ponder the mystery of the swirling hole,
A super-massive black abyss, devouring souls.
Through the depths of the universe, they delve,
Into the realms where the cosmic entities dwell,
A higher dimensional wormhole, they say,
Through which beings of darkness find their way.

Titans of unimaginable power and might,
Hidden from mortal sight, cloaked in the night,
They ingress and egress, their forms unseen,
Terror and madness, their only means.
They traverse the void, with malevolent intent,
Feeding on fear, on chaos, they are bent,
Astronomers shudder at the thought,
Of the horrors lurking, just beyond their ought.

Invisible to our eyes, but felt in the shadows

These cosmic entities, ancient and hollow
Ingress and egress through these portals of dread
Bringing chaos and destruction to all in their stead
They wander between realms, unchained and untamed
Leaving behind a trail of sorrow, of the damned
Their tendrils reaching out into the void
Corrupting all they touch, all they destroy

No prayer can save us from their wrath
No science can explain their path
We are but pawns in their cosmic game
And they play with us, without shame

Invisible to human eyes, these beings roam,
Capturing souls, dragging them into the unknown,
The cosmic fabric stretches and tears,
As the darkness engulfs, no one cares.
The stars flicker and fade, their light dim,
As the entities move, their presence grim,
The universe trembles in fear and dread,
As the astronomers ponder what lies ahead.

For in the depths of the blackened abyss,
The titanic, merciless entities hiss,
Their hunger unending, their power vast,
Astronomers realize, their fate is cast.
For in the end, we are but pawns,
In the game of the dark, where they spawn,
Through the wormholes, they come and go,
Invisible, untouchable, a never-ending shitshow.

34

Whispers

Whispers from the void, echoes in the night
A radio observatory, steeped in eerie light
Long-dead owners, trapped in a haunting plight
Their desperate attempts, to re-orient just right
Satellite dishes, pointed to the sky
But what they seek, they cannot identify
Something unseen, lurking in the cosmic expanse
Their last transmissions, a desperate dance

Ghostly voices, crackling through the air
Revealing their fear, their despair
The unknown force, tearing at their sanity
Their final plea, for an end to this calamity
A darkness encroaching, a chilling dread
Their efforts to escape, fall in line instead
Mercifully unseen, but felt in every bone
The owners of the observatory, forever alone.

TRISTA WOOJIN

| 72 |

35

Kilerth

Explorers venturing into the unknown expanse,
Discover a shimmering relic of the past,
The fossilized remains of a creature strange,
That defies the laws of logic and existence,
Non-Euclidean being, a puzzle for science,
Its form unfamiliar, a cosmic dance.

That should not biologically be, a dance,
This enigma stirs the minds of those who expound,
On the mysteries of life and the universe vast,
The creature's anatomy, a cryptic contrast,
To all known species, a challenge to science,
Unearthed from the ground, in the shadows cast.

According to the textbooks, this anomaly should not cast,
Its shadow on reality, a surreal dance,
A defiance of reason, a riddle for science,

How did this abomination come to exist?
In a world governed by rules so steadfast,
This non-Euclidean entity, so strange.

Its fossilized form whispers tales of the strange,
Of dimensions beyond, where shadows cast,
Illusions of normalcy, a barrier so steadfast,
Is shattered by the presence of this unworldly dance,
The explorers tremble at this twist in existence,
A conundrum that mocks the foundations of science.

They study the fossil with fervor, seeking answers in science,
But the truth remains elusive, the creature remains strange,
Its enigmatic origins a blight on their existence,
In the shadow of this mystery, doubts are cast,
Upon the very fabric of reality, a cosmic dance,
Of chaos and order, entangled in a dance so vast.

As the explorers delve deeper, the mysteries vast,
Of this non-Euclidean creation confound their science,
The dance of the entity, a cryptic romance,
With the paradoxes of being, so beautifully strange,
The shadows of doubt continue to be cast,
Over the foundations of their very existence.

In the fossilized remains of this non-Euclidean dance,
Explorers witness a truth so vast, beyond the reach of science,
An existence that defies reason, forever strange.

36

Warning

In the depths of a jungle valley, lost to time,
Lies a civilization shrouded in mystery and crime.
Their records speak of a science so advanced,
Drawing energies from a baby universe entranced.

In crystal-like hypergeometry, they found their power,
A dimension beyond our understanding, where they would shower
Themselves in the dark energies of the cosmos,
Feeding on the primal forces that few would dare to oppose.

But with this great power, came a terrible cost,
As the civilization fell into darkness, forever lost.
Their souls consumed by the malevolent energy,
Their bodies twisted and warped, a monstrous entity.

Now the valley lies silent, a graveyard of the past,
Where the echoes of madness and horror will forever last.
Beware those who dare to venture into the unknown,

For the secrets of this place are better left alone.

37

Voices of the Damned

The psychic mediums beckon
Channeling a deranged spirit, their souls stricken
With horror and dread, as the entity speaks
Inhuman coordinates, as darkness peaks
Whispers of warning, of a place unknown
A realm of terror, where the evil has grown
Do not dare to venture, do not cross that line
For in that cursed place, only death will find
The mediums tremble, their voices quiver
As the spirit's madness continues to deliver
A cryptic message, a prophecy of doom
Of a nightmare realm, where no light can loom

They cry out in despair, but the spirit persists
Repeating the coordinates, a twisted twist
In the fabric of space-time, a portal awaits
To a hellish dimension, where evil gate
The mediums are haunted, by visions so bleak
Of a world consumed by darkness, where the wicked seek

To devour the souls of those who dare to tread
In the forbidden land, where the spirits are dead
But still they chant, the unholy verse
The coordinates echoing, a curse
They try to resist, but the spirit is strong
Its malevolent presence, forever long

And so they are bound, to the whims of the dead
To the deranged spirit, filling them with dread
As they continue to channel, the same warning cry
Not to go to that place, where all hope will die
But the lure of the unknown, the call of the abyss
Begins to tempt them, a deadly kiss
They know the danger, the horrors that await
And yet, they are drawn to that forbidden gate
Will they heed the warnings, or succumb to temptation?
Will they brave the darkness, or flee in desperation?

Only time will tell, as they stand at the brink
Of a nightmare realm, where no light can link
The psychic mediums tremble, their fate uncertain
As they listen to the spirit's unholy sermon
Of inhuman coordinates, and warnings dire
Not to go to that place, where evil conspire.

38

Discovery in Siberia

In the desolate depths of Siberia's frozen land,
Unearthly transmissions are caught in the hand
Of amateur radio operators, bold and daring,
Their minds now exposed to nightmarish, unknowable blaring.
From unknown coordinates, the signals came,
A cryptic language, not meant for mortal frame,
They spoke of horrors beyond our comprehension,
Driving the listeners to the brink of ascension.
Decoding the messages, they found hidden truths,
Of ancient gods and forbidden occult roots,
The whispers of madness, creeping into their minds,
As they unearthed secrets of unspeakable kinds.

The infernal obscenities, too foul to transcribe,
Revealed a world where sanity could not abide,
They spoke of rituals and sacrifices so grotesque,
That the listeners trembled, fear at their necks.

Something ancient and malevolent was stirring,
In the shadows of Siberia, dark thoughts were whirring,
The radio operators, now haunted by their find,
Knew they had delved too deep, crossed a line.

But the transmissions continued, relentless and vile,
Each one a puzzle, each one a trial,
To decipher the madness, the code of the unknown,
To unlock the secrets of the throne.
As the signals grew stronger, the operators knew,
Their fate was sealed, their sanity askew,
For in deciphering the eldritch tongues of the void,
They had opened a door that could not be destroyed.

39

Bloodstained Paradise

Where wealth and privilege reign supreme,
A sinister shadow lurks in the darkness,
A serial squatter with a taste for blood.
They thought their fortress was impenetrable,
That the high walls and security guards,
Would keep out all harm and danger,
But they were wrong, oh so very wrong.

On a moonlit night, the squatter struck,
Silent as a ghost, he crept through the shadows,
Leaving a trail of bodies in his wake,
A chilling reminder of their false sense of security.
The residents awoke to screams and sirens,
Panic and fear gripped their hearts,
As they realized the truth of their situation,
Safety was now the illusion...danger the new reality.
No longer could they hide behind their gates,
No longer could they pretend to be untouchable,
For the darkness had come for them,

And there was nowhere left to run.

Their once perfect paradise now stained with blood,
Their pristine walls now tainted with fear,
The price of their ignorance and arrogance,
A heavy toll that could not be undone.
So as the sun sets on the once elite community,
And the shadows grow long and deep,
Remember that darkness can touch us all,
And safety is but a fleeting illusion

40

Xerxes

As humankind expands its reach into the stars
A new extremist political faction emerges
Waging war to keep planets "pure" of alien and robot inhabitants
Led by a figure shrouded in shadows

His name is Xerxes, a man of great power and influence
A charismatic leader with a twisted vision
Of a universe free from the contamination
Of beings not born of human flesh
He preaches hate and fear to his followers
Promising a purer future for their children

Under his command, the faction grows
Fueled by propaganda and violence
They strike out at any non-human presence
On the planets they seek to claim
Their ships soar through the void
Leaving destruction in their wake

Xerxes, with his icy gaze and cold heart
Seeks to erase all traces of the alien
To make the cosmos a mirror of humanity
But as he wages his war, he becomes a monster
His once noble cause twisted by hatred
Into a brutal and merciless crusade

The screams of the innocent echo through the void
As Xerxes and his followers lay waste
To all that is not human
Their hearts hardened by their twisted beliefs
They see only enemies in the stars
And seek to cleanse the universe of their presence

But as they march onward, sowing destruction
They fail to see the true enemy
The darkness that lurks within
Their own souls, corrupted by fear and hate
Xerxes, once a man of vision and purpose
Now a puppet of his own twisted ideology

And as the war rages on, consuming planets
And civilizations in its wake
Xerxes stands at the head of his faction
A twisted king ruling over a kingdom of ash and blood
But in the end, even he will see
That his war has only brought ruin and despair

For in the darkness of space, there is no place
For those consumed by hatred and fear
And Xerxes, once a man of power and influence

Will be left alone in the void
A broken shell of his former self

41

Waiting For The Stars To Align

Upon death, the powerful clerics are laid to rest,
Their bodies embalmed in a ritual so profane,
Their consciousness preserved in mummified remains,
Awaiting the moment when the stars align,
And they may be awakened once again,
To continue their duties in the secret religious order.

These clerics, bound by their sacred order,
Know that even in death, they are not truly at rest,
For their souls are trapped within their mummified remains,
Subjected to a fate most dark and profane,
Their minds aching for the day when the stars align,
And they are free once more to walk among men.

For centuries they lie dormant, waiting for the stars to align,
Their bodies preserved, their spirits bound to the order,
Each night haunted by visions so profane,
Of a world they cannot touch, a rest they cannot find,
Their existence a cruel joke, their souls trapped in remains,

Their only solace the hope of awakening again.

But the years pass, and still the stars refuse to align,
The clerics growing restless in their mummified remains,
Their minds consumed by darkness, their spirits strained,
The weight of eternity pressing down on their order,
Their once sacred duties now a source of profane,
Their souls longing for release, for eternal rest.

And so they suffer, trapped in their mummified remains,
Their minds fractured, their spirits broken, their hopes of awakening dashed,
With each passing year, the stars seem further from align,
Their existence a torture, their order a curse so profane,
Their only solace the thought of a final rest,
The sweet release of death from their eternal rest.

But still they endure, bound to their profane fate,
Their bodies mummified, their minds in a restless state,
Their order forgotten, their souls in agony,
As they wait in darkness for the stars to align,
And grant them release from their mummified remains—
A final end to their eternal rest.

So here they lie, the clerics of the secret order,
Their bodies mummified, their souls in torment,
Awaiting the moment when the stars align,
And they may be awakened once again,
To continue their duties in a world so dark and profane,
Trapped forever in their mummified remains.

42

Barkamsted

Solitary
Probe drifts through silence
Xenoforms of nightmare
In the dark void between stars
Probe's doom foretold, lost

Whispers echo
Abyssal thoughts entwine
The alien probe's mind
Overloading, cracking firewalls
Darkness consumes all

Gargantuan
Monsters lurk and writhe
In the depths of space
Their presence a cosmic threat
Probing minds, twisted

Telemetry
Reveals the horror
Of the void's true nature
Alien probe meets its end
In the abyssal deep

Lost to darkness
No trace of the probe remains
Xenoforms victorious
Their secrets untold
In the vast unknown

43

Halivaara

As astronomers delve into the depths of time
Searching for clues in the relic neutrino radiation
Uncovering the secrets of the universe's creation
They stumble upon a truth too dark to comprehend
Triggered by events from a distant cosmic inflation

Across the fabric of time, echoes of inflation
Reverberate through the void where darkness reigns
Astronomers unravel the mystery, their minds unable to comprehend
The implications of artificially triggered events in space and time
Encoded within the relic radiation
Whispers of a past that defies explanation

Nonlocal signatures, a cryptic communication
From a time before time, a cosmic inflation
The fingerprints of a force beyond comprehension
Unraveling the tapestry where darkness reigns
Astronomers confront the limits of their understanding of time

As they grapple with the implications of the radiation

The universe unfolds, a symphony of creation
Pulled from the void by the hand of inflation
Astronomers gaze into the abyss, their minds racing through time
To grasp the meaning behind the cosmic communication
Encoded within the relic radiation
They unearth a truth so dark, it shatters their comprehension

Across the eons, the echoes of inflation
Reverberate through the darkness, a cosmic revelation
Astronomers confront a reality beyond their comprehension
Triggered by events that defy explanation
Through the relic radiation, they decode the communication
Connecting the dots across the vast expanse of time

In the blackness of space, a darkness reigns
As astronomers probe the mysteries of time
Unraveling the secrets of cosmic inflation
And the fingerprints of creation left in the relic radiation
They grapple with a truth so dark, it defies comprehension
An artificially triggered big bang echoing through the epochs

As time unfolds, the astronomers gaze into the void
Seeking to comprehend the cosmic communication
Encoded within the relic radiation, a symphony of creation
Revealing the secrets of cosmic inflation
And the echoes of events triggered in the darkness
A truth so dark, it transcends all understanding

In the depths of space, the darkness reigns

As astronomers confront the enigma of time
Unraveling the cosmic inflation
And decoding the relic radiation's ancient communication

44 ▍

Unfair Games

Corruption reigns supreme,
Innocence is a currency,
And justice just a dream.

They thought the stories exaggerated,
The whispers of a dark trade,
But then they stumbled upon a ring,
Of children bought and sold like wares.

The world turned a blind eye,
To the horrors lurking in the dark,
But now they must face the truth,
And ignite a flame in their hearts.

No more can they sit idly by,
As the world turns a blind eye,
They must rise against the darkness,
And fight for those who can't cry.

But the road ahead is treacherous,
Filled with danger and despair,
For the enemies they face are cunning,
And they play a game unfair.

Against ruthless warlords they must stand,
And corrupted politicians too,
Their only weapons are their hearts,
And the courage to see it through.

So they play a game of chess,
With the lives of children at stake,
And in the shadows of the night,
They fight for justice's sake.

But the darkness is relentless,
And the battle seems in vain,
They must keep the flame burning,
Or their efforts will wane.

For in a world where corruption reigns supreme,
It takes a spark of hope,
To shatter the darkest dream.

45 ▌

The Poisoned Pen

There lurks a dark presence, a poison unseen
The Poison Pen letters, like daggers they fly
Exposing the secrets of those high and nigh
Wealthy elite, with their silk and their gold
Their lives are unraveling, their secrets unfold
The pen spares no mercy, it holds no fear

It whispers of death, it brings terror near
The powerful tremble, their sins on display
Their carefully crafted facades now decay
Blackmail and treachery, all laid bare
The Poison Pen's justice, they can't repair
A web of vengeance, woven tight

The city's fate hangs in the balance of night
For if the culprit remains free
Who knows what darkness we'll soon see
So heed this warning, all who read
The Poison Pen's wrath is born of greed

Beware the shadows, watch your back

For the city's fate rests on this dark track
The mystery deepens, the stakes grow high
As the Poison Pen's letters continue to fly
Will justice prevail, or will darkness reign
Only time will tell, in this web of pain
So lock your doors, and guard your heart

For the Poison Pen's venom seeps through the start
The city's elite, their downfall draws near
As the Poison Pen whispers, their end is here.

www.ingramcontent.com/pod-product-compliance
Lightning Source LLC
Chambersburg PA
CBHW040152160726
48006CB00014B/1719